WHERE'S THE ROYAL FAMILY?

A REGAL SEARCH AND FIND BOOK

ORCHARD

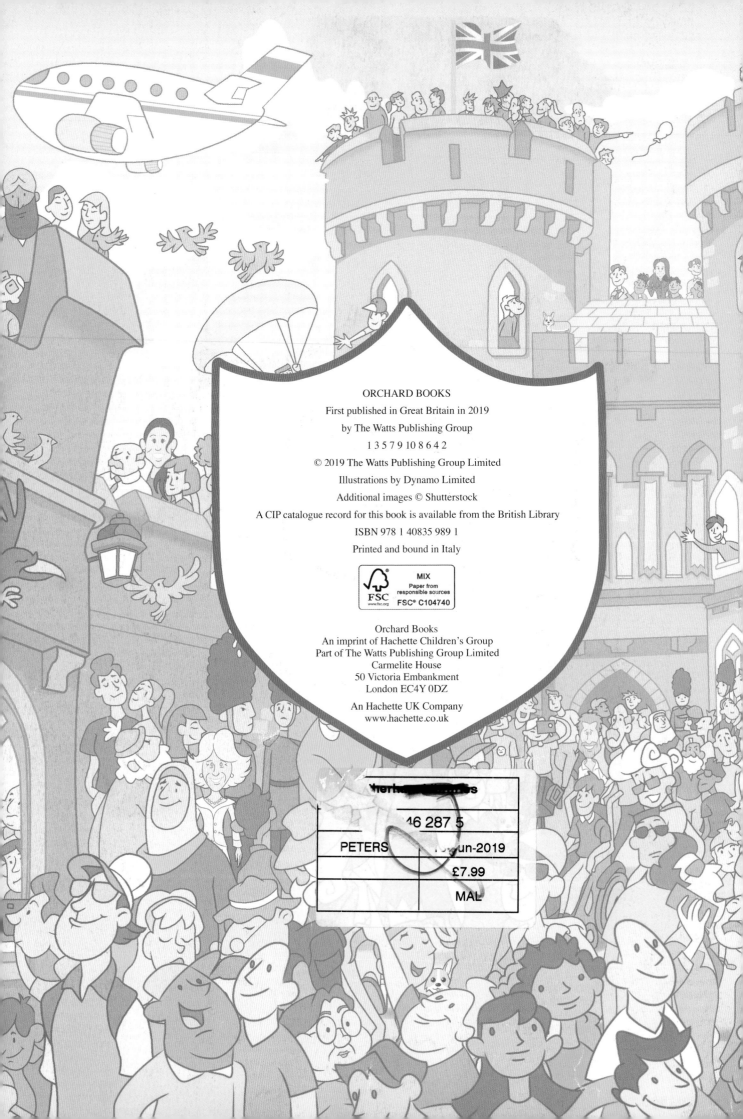

ORCHARD BOOKS

First published in Great Britain in 2019

by The Watts Publishing Group

1 3 5 7 9 10 8 6 4 2

© 2019 The Watts Publishing Group Limited

Illustrations by Dynamo Limited

Additional images © Shutterstock

A CIP catalogue record for this book is available from the British Library

ISBN 978 1 40835 989 1

Printed and bound in Italy

MIX
Paper from
responsible sources
FSC® C104740
FSC
www.fsc.org

Orchard Books
An imprint of Hachette Children's Group
Part of The Watts Publishing Group Limited
Carmelite House
50 Victoria Embankment
London EC4Y 0DZ

An Hachette UK Company
www.hachette.co.uk

WHERE'S THE ROYAL FAMILY?

A REGAL SEARCH AND FIND BOOK

A RIGHT ROYAL ADVENTURE!

The British royal family holds the crown as one of the world's most famous and well loved dynasties. They travel the world carrying out their royal duties, visiting exciting locations and meeting lots of new people!

Join the royals on a very special trip, and try to spot them on their travels. The Queen is taking her beloved corgis – there are 10 to find in every picture. A royal baby makes a special appearance in one place, too! If you get stuck, you can find the answers at the back of the book.

THE QUEEN

Queen Elizabeth II has been on the throne even longer than her famous ancestor, Queen Victoria. The Queen loves animals, and was once given an elephant as an official gift!

CAMILLA

The Duchess of Cornwall is patron of over 90 charities, including an animal rescue home from which she adopted two Jack Russell terriers.

PRINCE CHARLES

Prince Charles is heir to the throne. As well as his duties as Prince of Wales, Charles is a writer, farmer and organic-food producer – and once appeared in a TV soap opera!

CORGIS

The Queen adores corgis! **Look out for 10 of her canine companions in every picture.**

BABY

Everyone loves a royal baby! Can you spot the newest addition to the royal family on their first adventure?

MEGHAN

The Duchess of Sussex brings a dose of Hollywood glamour to the royal family. When she came to England she brought her canine companions with her.

PRINCE HARRY

Prince Harry has served as a soldier, and is a passionate campaigner and adventurer. He once trekked all the way across Antarctica to the South Pole.

PRINCE PHILIP

Prince Philip is the oldest member of the royal family. He is enjoying his retirement, having carried out over 22,000 official engagements in his lifetime.

KATE

Catherine, also known as Kate, met Prince William at university, where she walked the runway in a fashion show. She is now a global fashion icon, and she also loves playing sport!

PRINCE WILLIAM

Prince William is second in line to the throne. When he served as a helicopter pilot in a search and rescue team his nickname was 'Billy the Fish' – a pun on his name, William Wales.

HOME SWEET HOME

The royal family is gathering at Buckingham Palace, the Queen's home in London. They're going on a world tour and they can't wait to start planning which countries to visit!

Can you spot all the royals ready for an adventure?

LOOK BUT DON'T TOUCH

The royal palaces are filled with treasures that the Queen and her ancestors have collected through the ages – everyone has to take care not to knock anything over!

Find all the family members amongst the precious items.

NEAREST AND DEER-EST

At Balmoral Castle in Scotland everyone enjoys the fresh air and outdoor pursuits. Look, is that the Loch Ness monster?

Grab your binoculars to find the Queen and her family enjoying their holiday.

ON THE SLOPES

Brrr! It's cold in the mountains, but everyone is having fun in the snow – skiing, snowboarding, sledging, or just admiring the beautiful scenery. Watch out for the yeti!

Can you spot the royals in the wintry scene?

NEW YORK, NEW YORK

The royal family has come to the USA, and Meghan can't wait to show everyone around the famous sights of Manhattan, from the Statue of Liberty to the Empire State Building. All aboard!

Find all the family members before they head downtown.

LET THE GOOD TIMES ROLL

A trip to the theatre or a spot of shopping? There's so much to do in New York, but the Queen can't wait to let her corgis loose for a run around Central Park.

Can you find the royals in all the hustle and bustle of Times Square?

THE WILD SIDE

ROARRRRR! The royals are on safari.
There are so many amazing animals to see in
their natural habitat. Don't get too close!

Can you see all the royals hidden amongst the animals?

G'DAY FROM THE BAY

The royal family has come Down Under!
They're visiting the famous Sydney Opera House
and taking a spin round the harbour.

Can you find each royal as they bask in the sunshine?

LET THE GAMES BEGIN

The royals are cheering on the athletes in a big sports event. They're not taking part in the races, but they're having their own competition to see who can cheer the loudest!

Can you find all the royals in the stadium?

MAKING WAVES

The royal family has arrived back in London and the crowds have turned out to welcome them. The Queen has her famous wave ready for the occasion!

Can you find each member of the royal family in amongst all the well-wishers?

CLOCKING OFF

They're nearly home! The Queen has some official duties at the Houses of Parliament, while the rest of the family enjoys messing about on the river.

Can you spot them before Big Ben strikes the hour?

TIME FOR TEA

The Queen has invited lots of people to a garden party. There are cups of tea, dainty sandwiches and plenty of sweet treats for all to enjoy.

Can you find the royals having a whale of a time?

LET'S DANCE

The royal family is celebrating the end of their world tour with a grand party. They love visiting different countries and meeting interesting people – but there's no place like home!

Can you spot them dancing the night away with their happy guests?

Now try and find these extra items in every scene!

HOME SWEET HOME

A man holding an ice cream cone ☐

A person playing the xylophone ☐

A boy eating a hot dog ☐

Three green flowers ☐

A child in a pushchair ☐

A half-eaten sandwich ☐

A woman with a flag ☐

A man having his photo taken ☐

A girl stroking a horse ☐

A man using a telephone box ☐

LOOK BUT DON'T TOUCH

A dog's bone ☐

A camera flash ☐

The number seven ☐

A yellow earring ☐

A man wearing a scarf ☐

A girl with a backpack ☐

A sleeping cat ☐

A lamp ☐

Two burning candles ☐

A cushion ☐

CASTLE ON THE HILL

A yellow balloon ☐

A dog with a sceptre ☐

A girl wearing a crown ☐

A man in a car ☐

A girl in a blue skirt ☐

A fallen ice cream cone ☐

A T-shirt with a smiley face ☐

A man with a brown beard ☐

A person talking on the phone ☐

Some blue flowers ☐

NEAREST AND DEER-EST

A bird with an orange beak ☐

A person with a camera ☐

A woman pointing ☐

Five golf balls ☐

A woman with a walking stick ☐

A yellow and red kite ☐

A dog with a blue collar ☐

A person with blue hair ☐

A man with a red tie ☐

A person with matching gloves, hat and scarf ☐

ON THE SLOPES

A yeti ☐

Someone with different coloured skis ☐

A pile of snowballs ☐

A person with an orange scarf ☐

A cat ☐

Somebody stuck in the snow ☐

A bird with a red beak ☐

A snowman ☐

Two pink skis ☐

A person with a green helmet ☐

NEW YORK, NEW YORK

A fish ☐

A red flag ☐

A man with green hair ☐

Someone wearing sunglasses ☐

A man holding a drink ☐

A capsized boat ☐

A woman in a blue dress ☐

A tower with five windows ☐

A spaceship ☐

A man with a walking stick ☐

LET THE GOOD TIMES ROLL

A hot dog ☐

A blue camera ☐

A feather ☐

A man with earphones ☐

Someone riding a horse ☐

A man with a red hat ☐

A cookie ☐

A heart ☐

Someone dressed as the
Statue of Liberty ☐

A fire hydrant ☐

THE WILD SIDE

A crocodile ☐

Three butterflies ☐

Two bananas ☐

A snake ☐

Eight blue birds ☐

Seven giraffes ☐

Three pink birds ☐

Six elephants ☐

An eagle ☐

Seven monkeys ☐

G'DAY FROM THE BAY

A floating bottle ☐

A red flag ☐

A woman with a green headband ☐

A red car ☐

An anchor ☐

A megaphone ☐

A seagull ☐

A mermaid with pink hair ☐

A woman in an orange T-shirt ☐

A pink star ☐

LET THE GAMES BEGIN

A mascot ☐

A man sitting down with a clipboard ☐

A blue and yellow water bottle ☐

A woman with a pink hat ☐

A person wearing a red helmet ☐

A woman holding medals ☐

A boom microphone ☐

A man with a green tie ☐

A sports bag ☐

A person doing shot put ☐

MAKING WAVES

- The London Eye ☐
- The letter 'H' ☐
- A woman with a microphone ☐
- A teddy bear ☐
- A man with blue hair ☐
- A woman with a yellow headscarf ☐
- A man chasing after a dog ☐
- A dog with its bone ☐
- A man with a pink hat ☐
- A horse eating flowers ☐

CLOCKING OFF

- A woman with an umbrella ☐
- A man with a red swimming cap ☐
- A mermaid ☐
- A man with a green hat ☐
- Someone scuba diving ☐
- A woman with pink hair ☐
- A yellow inflatable dinghy ☐
- Someone fishing ☐
- Seven lifesaver rings ☐
- A flag ☐

TIME FOR TEA

Someone holding a teacup ☐

A woman wearing gloves ☐

Two men with monocles ☐

A purple umbrella ☐

A woman wearing an orange skirt ☐

A man being chased by a swan ☐

A woman wearing a green hat ☐

Some yellow flowers ☐

A woman with a tray of sandwiches ☐

Two yellow birds ☐

LET'S DANCE

A woman in a yellow top ☐

A lost shoe ☐

Fallen sheet music ☐

A woman with a bow on her dress ☐

A person wearing an apron ☐

A statue of a man ☐

Seven potted plants ☐

A person playing the cello ☐

Two empty trays ☐

Someone who has lost their glasses ☐